0056615

S0-BSE-316

DATE DUE

MAR 2 7 1992	MAR 1 9 1997
APR. 1 3 1993	JUL 1 5 1997
MAY 1 2 1994	
FEB 1 5	OCT 0 2 1997
MAY 2 8 1996	OCT 2 0 1997
	NOV 1 4 1997
DEC 05 1996	DEC 08 1997

NB
623
B9
H86
1975

Michelangelo
Buonarroti, 1475-
1564.

Pieta.

$6.95

© THE BAKER & TAYLOR CO.

MICHELANGELO

PIETÀ

150 Photographs and Commentary
by
ROBERT HUPKA

Photographs and Text © 1975 by Robert Hupka
except the two photographs on page 76 by Wide World Photos, Inc.

Library of Congress Catalogue Card Number: 75-13645
ISBN: O 517 524147

I am grateful to Stefan Salter who has helped me with this book.

First Printing, 1975—25,000 copies
Second Printing, 1979—19,000 copies
Third Printing, 1984—26,000 copies

Published simultaneously in Canada by General Publishing Company Limited.

DESIGN AND PRODUCTION BY ROBERT HUPKA
Set in Palatino by Towne Typographers, Inc., New York
Printed in Stonetone by Rapoport Printing Corp., New York
Bound by Bookbinders, Inc., Jersey City, New Jersey

TO

MICHELANGELO

1475 · 1975

CONTENTS

INDICE

TABLE DES MATIÈRES

The Pietà is the only work of Michelangelo on which he incised his name. Giorgio Vasari, his biographer and contemporary, relates that one day Michelangelo was in St. Peter's when a group of visitors from Lombardy greatly admired his Pietà and he heard one of them say that the artist was: *our Hunchback of Milan.* Michelangelo returned at night with a lantern and carved in Latin on the band across the Virgin's robe:

MICHELANGELO BUONARROTI, THE FLORENTINE, MADE IT

La Pietà est le seul ouvrage de Michel-Ange qui porte sa signature. Giorgio Vasari, biographe et contemporain de Michel-Ange, reconte qu'un jour Michel-Ange, étant à Saint-Pierre, entendit un groupe de visiteurs de Lombardie qui admiraient sa Pietà. L'un d'entre eux disait que l'artiste était: *notre bossu de Milan.* Michel-Ange revint la nuit avec une lanterne et grava en latin dans le ruban de la robe de la Vierge:

MICHELANGELO BUONARROTI, DE FLORENCE, L'A SCULPTEE

La Pietá es la única de las obras de Miguel Angel en la que él puso su nombre. Giorgio Vasari, su biógrafo y contemporáneo, relata que estando un día Miguel Angel en San Pedro encontró a un grupo de visitantes procedentes de Lombardía admirando elogiosamente su Pietá. El oyó a uno de ellos diciendo que el artista era: *nuestro jorobado de Milán.* Miguel Angel regresó por la noche con una linterna y grabó en latín sobre la cinta que cruza el ropaje de la Virgen:

MICHELANGELO BUONARROTI, EL FLORENTINO, LA HIZO

La Pietà è l'unica opera di Michelangelo sulla quale incise il suo nome. Secondo Giorgio Vasari, biografo e contemporaneo di Michelangelo, un giorno in San Pietro Michelangelo s'imbattè in un gruppo di Lombardi che ammiravano molto la sua Pietà e sentì che uno di essi diceva che l'artista era: *il Gobbo nostro da Milano.* Michelangelo ritornò di notte con una lanterna e scolpì in latino sulla striscia che attraversa la veste della Vergine:

MICHELANGELO BUONARROTI, FIORENTINO, FECE

Die Pietà ist das einzige Werk Michelangelos, auf das er seinen Namen setzte. Giorgio Vasari, sein zeitgenössischer Biograph, erzählt, dass Michelangelo eines Tages in der Peterskirche war, als eine Gruppe von Besuchern aus der Lombardei seine Pietà sehr bewunderte, und er hörte, als einer von ihnen sagte, der Bildhauer sei: *unser Buckliger aus Mailand.* Michelangelo kehrte bei Nacht mit einer Laterne zurück und meisselte in Latein in das Band, das quer über das Gewand der Jungfrau läuft:

MICHELANGELO BUONARROTI, DER FLORENTINER, MACHTE SIE

A Pietà é a única obra em que Miguel Angelo gravou seu nome. Giorgio Vasari, seu biógrafo e contemporâneo, conta que um dia Miguel Angelo se encontrava na Basílica de São Pedro quandro um grupo de pessoas de Lombardia admiravam muito a Pietà e ouviu uma delas dizer que o artista era: *nosso corcunda de Milão.* Miguel Angelo voltou de noite com uma lanterna e gravou em latim na faixa que cruza o vestido da Virgem:

MIGUEL ANGELO BUONARROTI, O FLORENTINO, A FEZ

MICHAEL·AGLVS·BONAROTVS·FLOEN·FACEBA

MICHAEL·ANGELUS·BONAROTUS·FLORENTINUS·FACIEBA(T)

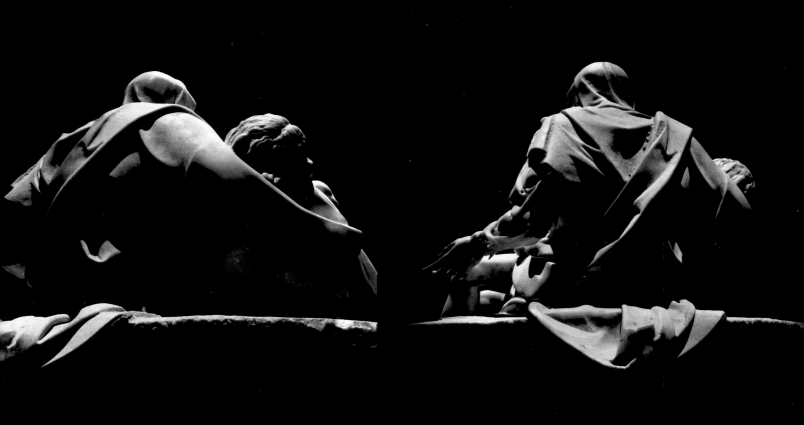

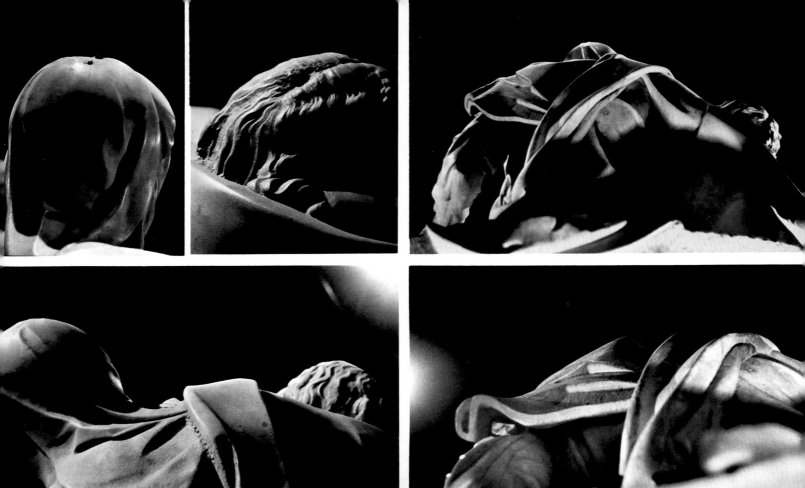

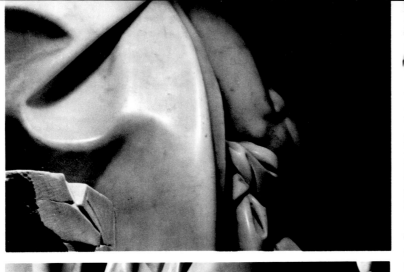

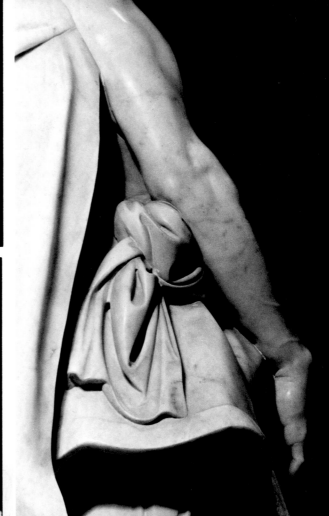

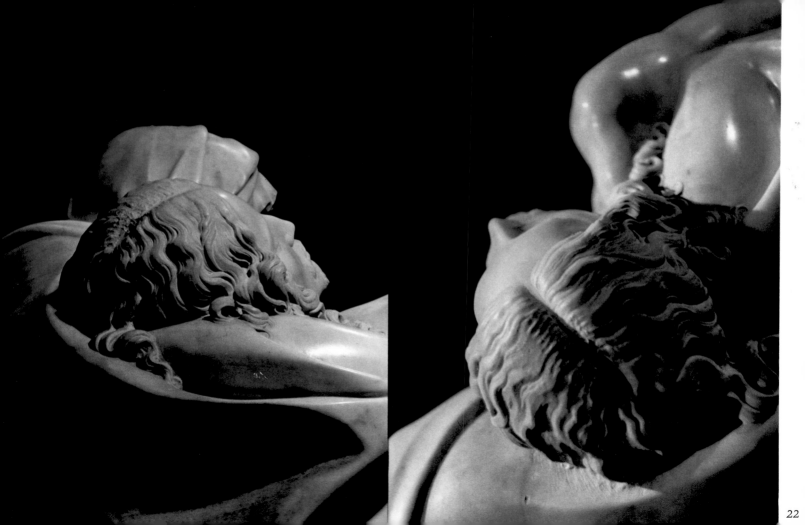

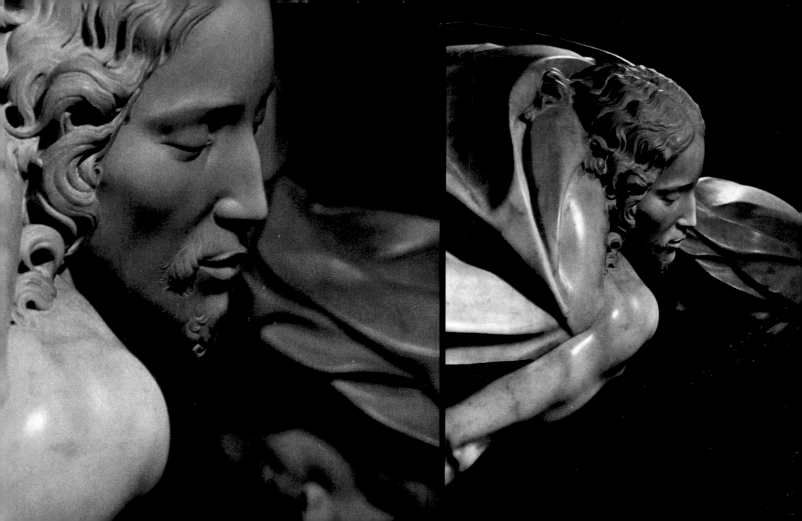

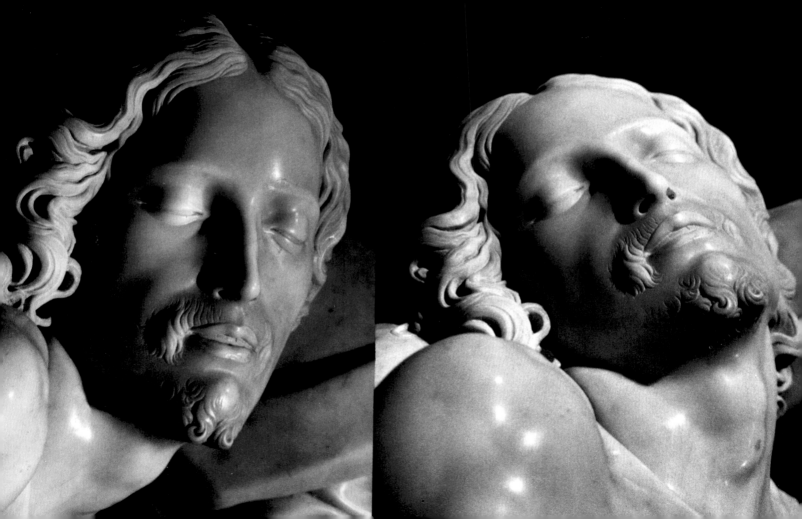

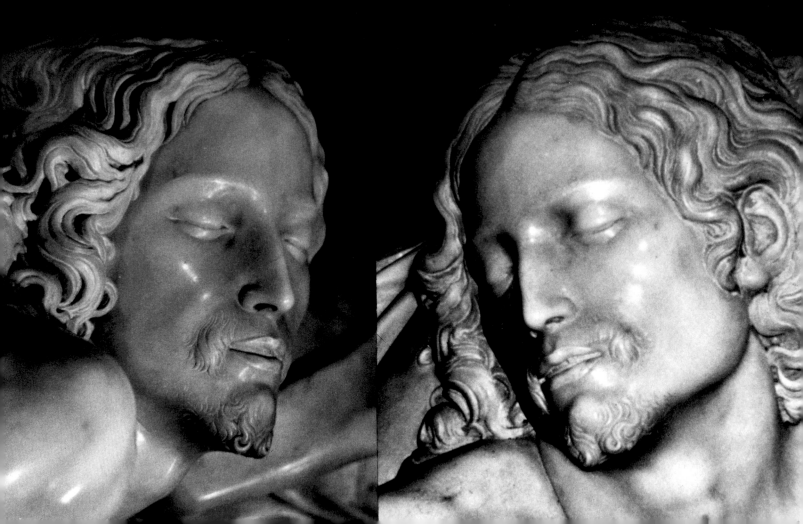

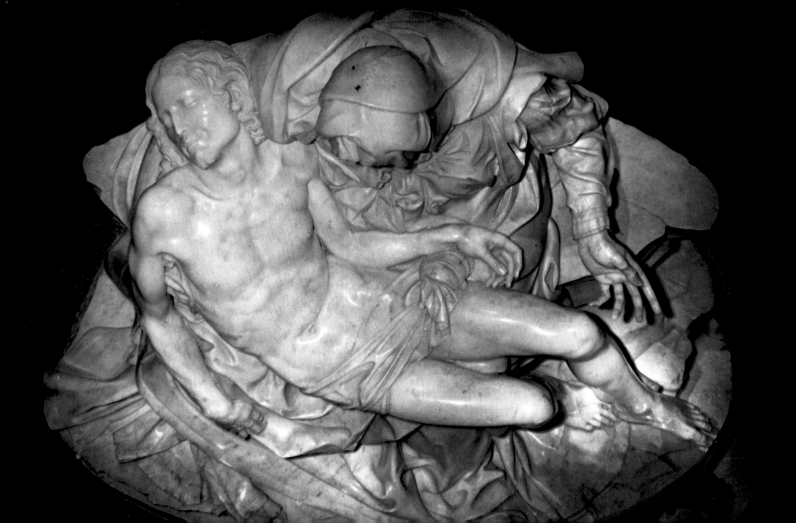

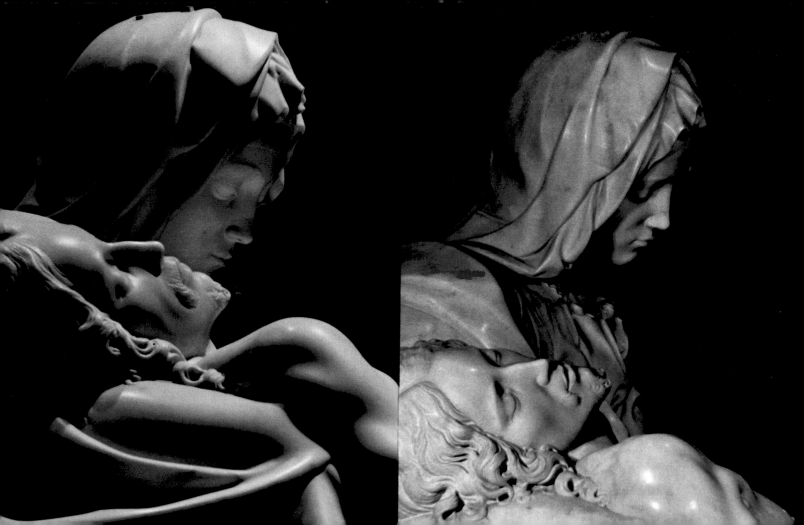

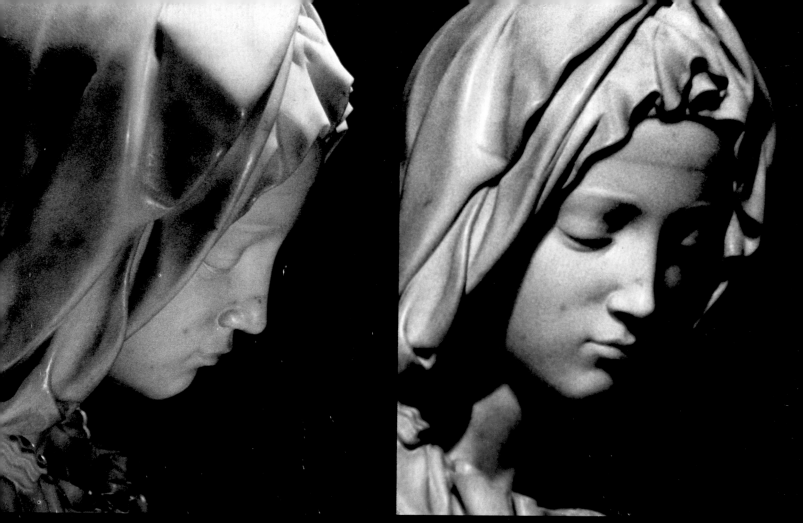

46

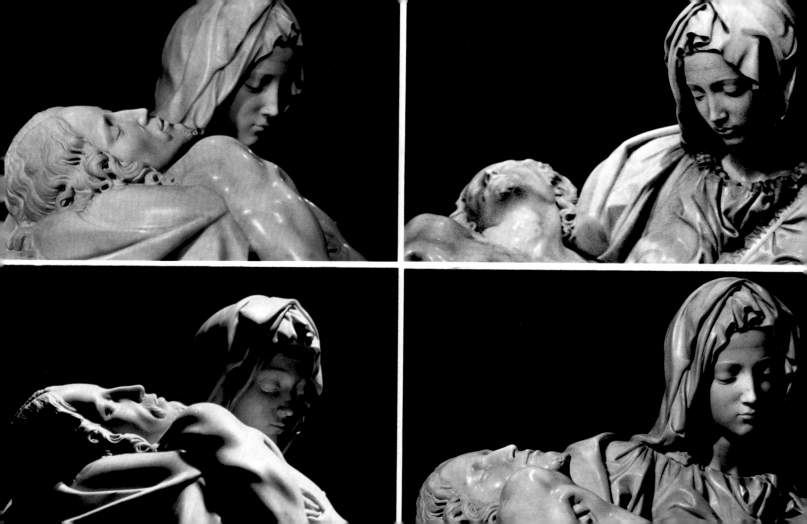

II

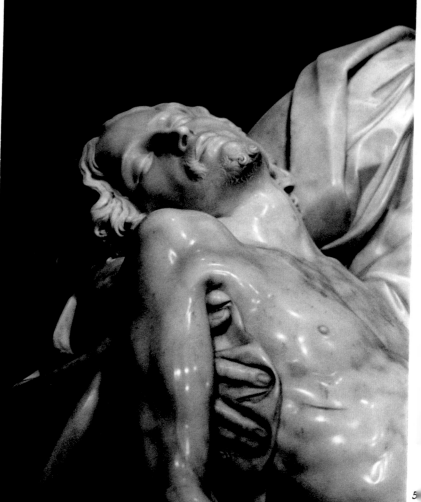

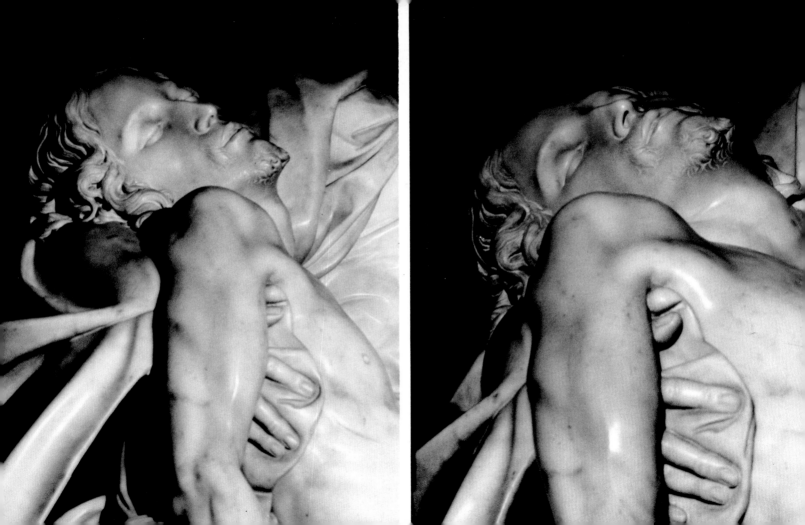

52

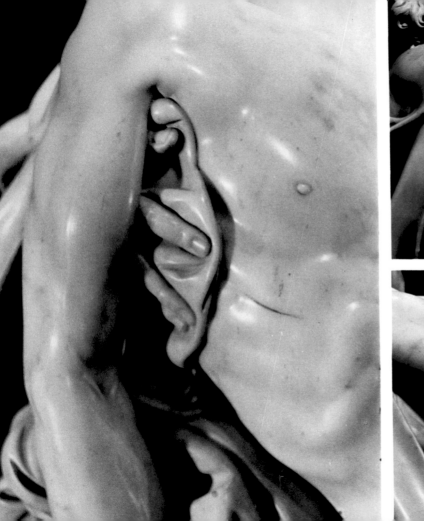

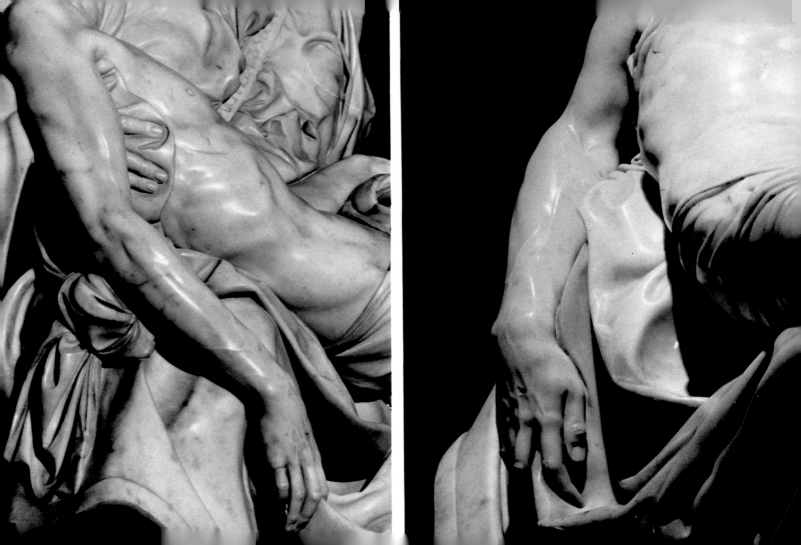

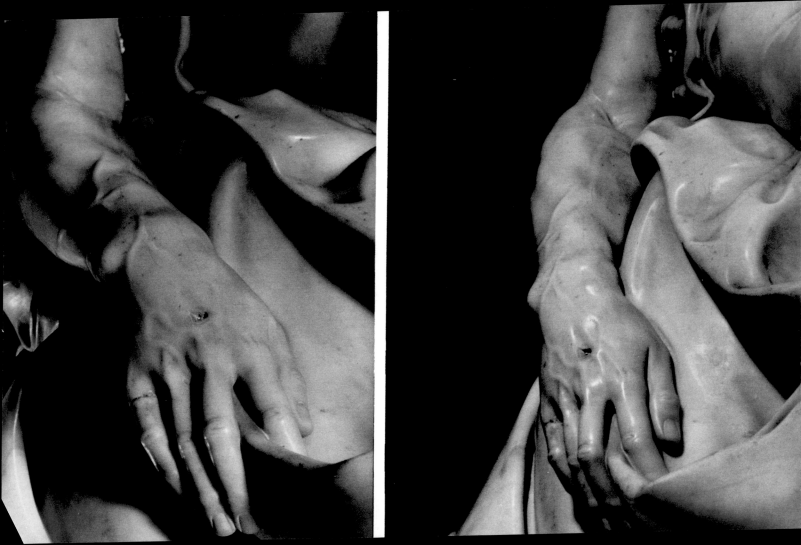

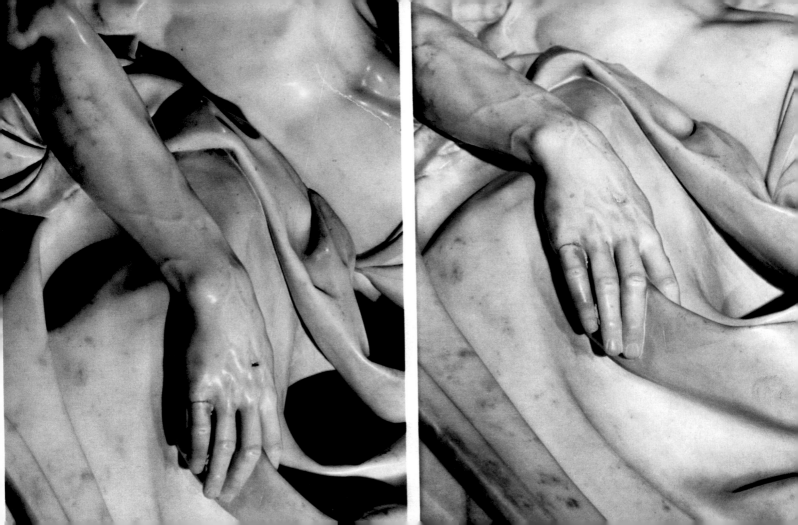

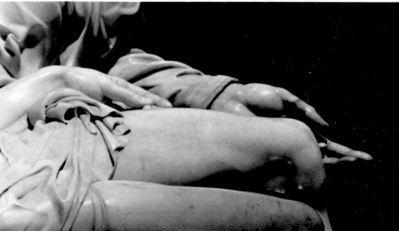

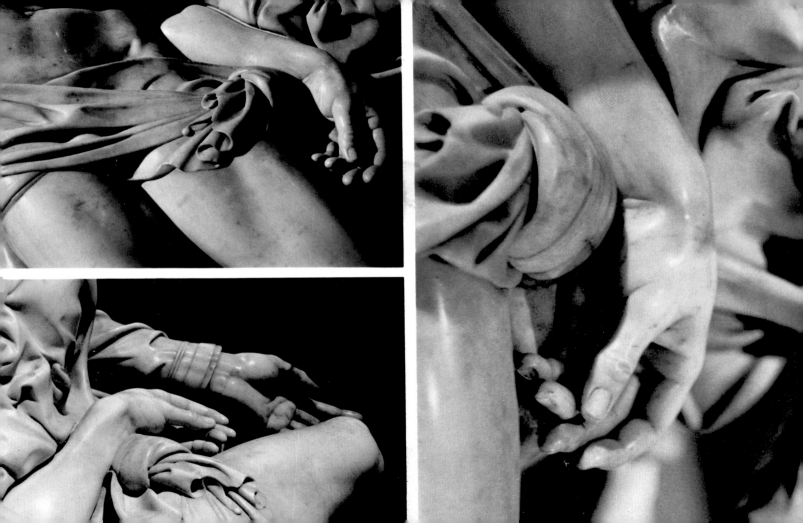

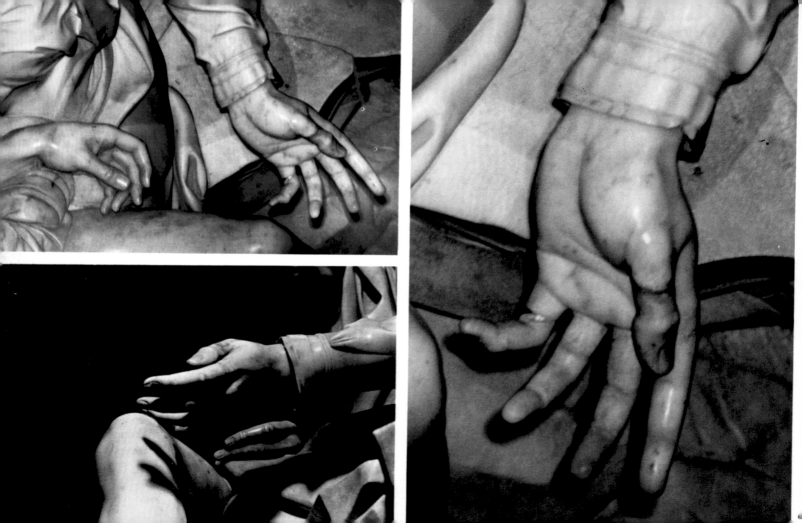

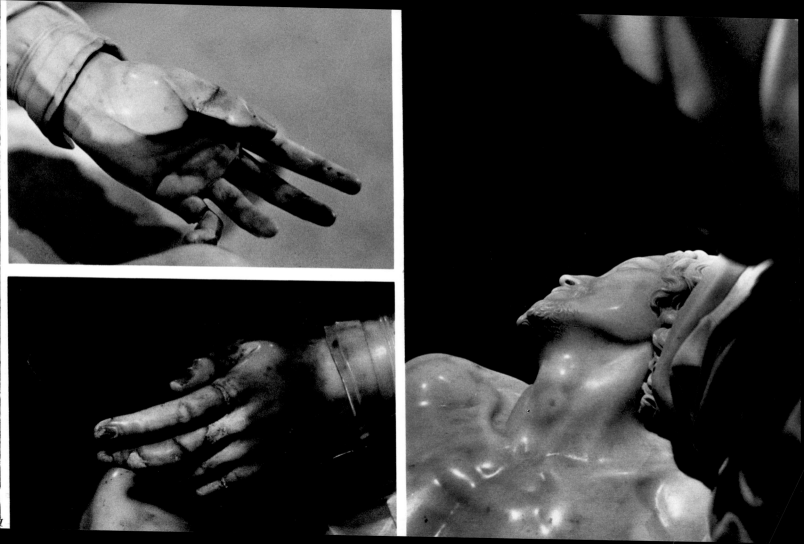

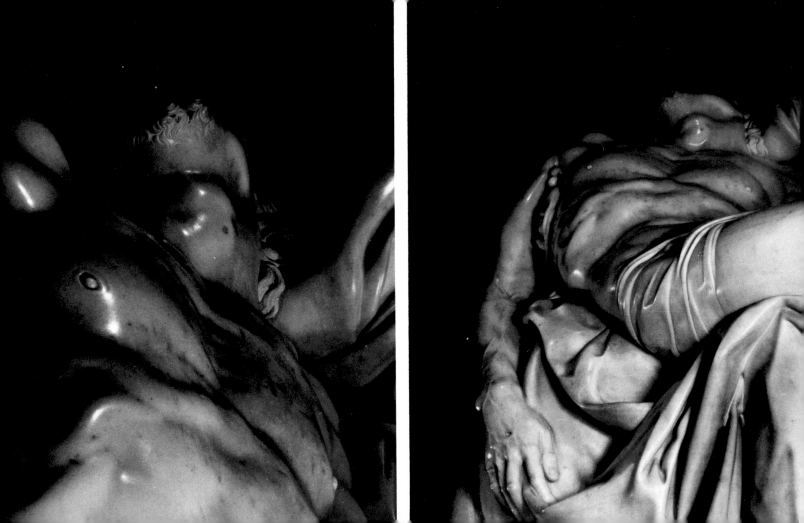

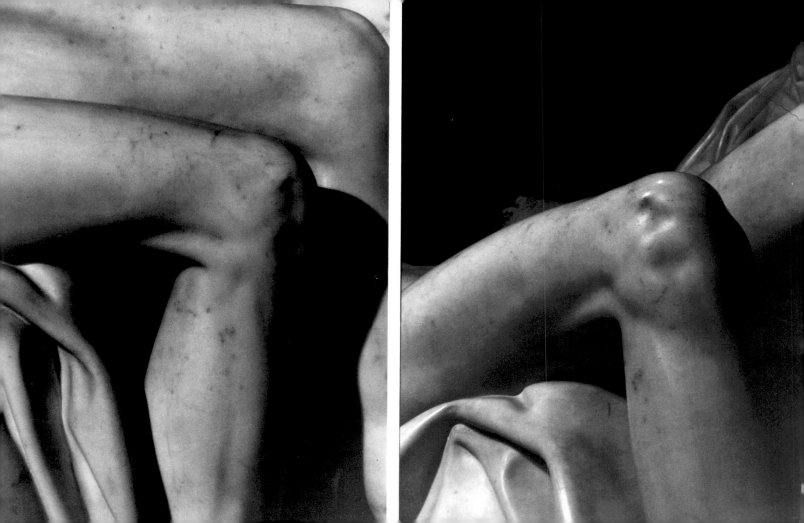

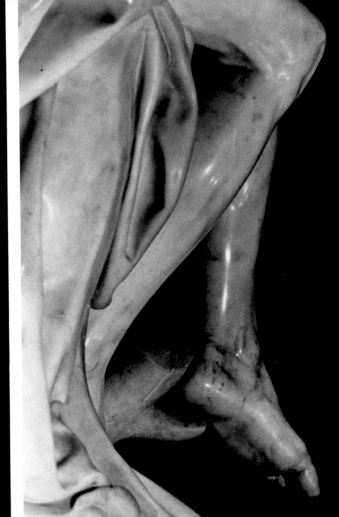

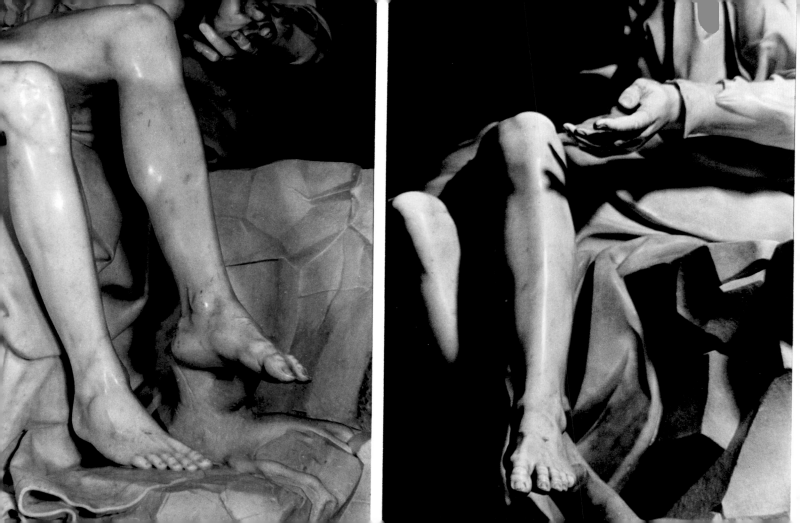

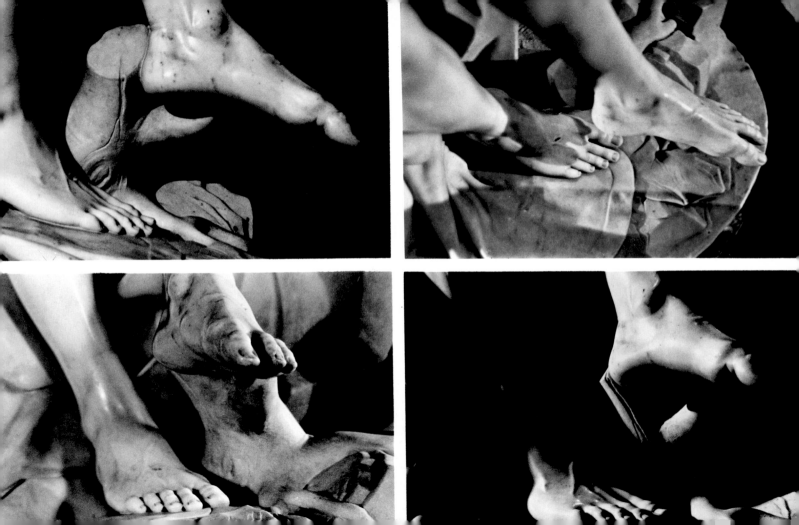

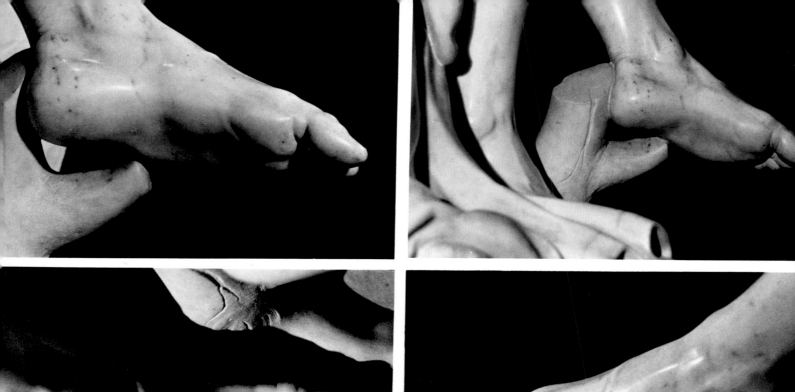

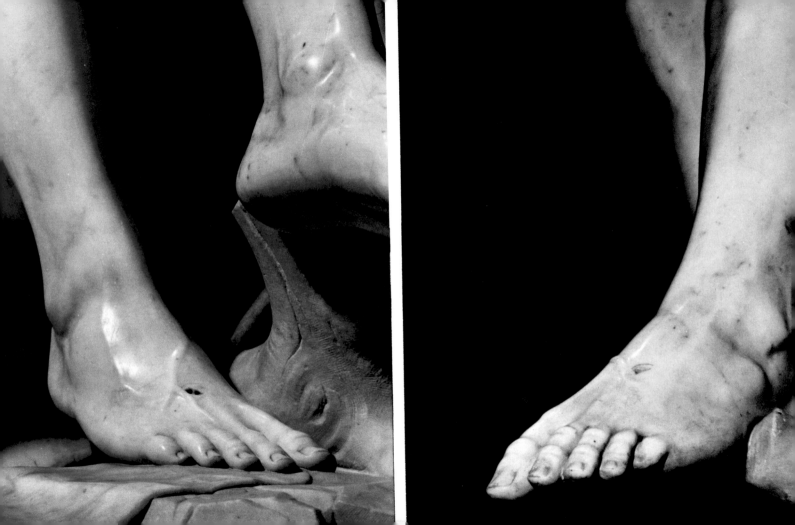

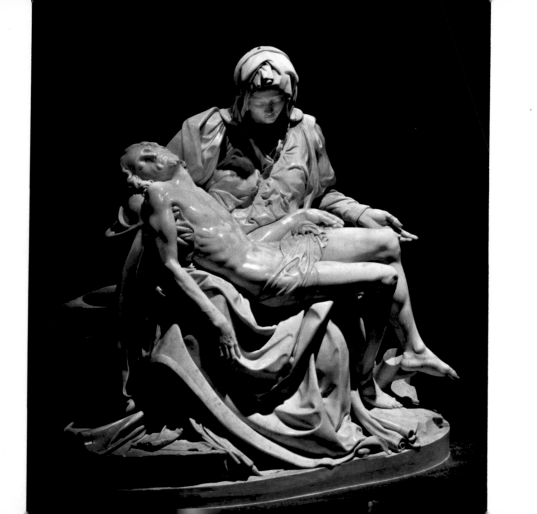

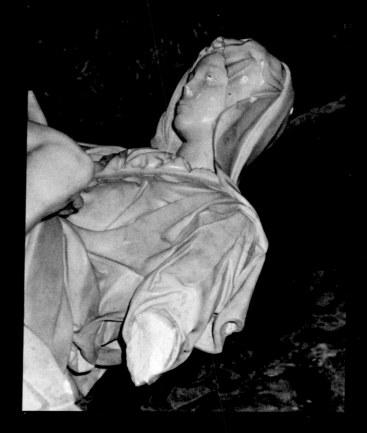

THE PIETÀ

Pietà, an Italian word meaning "pity," "compassion," "sorrow," is derived from the Latin *pietas*, signifying "loyalty to the highest degree . . . a profound love that neither life nor death can destroy." The classic meaning of the word *pietà* is the whole-souled abiding in the Divine Will, but it is also the name traditionally given to works of art representing the dead body of Christ in the arms of His Mother.

HISTORICAL DATA

Michelangelo Buonarroti, who was born in Caprese, near Florence, on March 6, 1475, and died in Rome on February 18, 1564, sculptured four Pietàs. This book is devoted to the first and most famous of them. The 68.5-inch-high statue, carved from one block of white Carrara marble, was commissioned by Cardinal Jean de Bilhères de Lagraulas of St. Denis, French Ambassador to the Holy See, for the Chapel of the Kings of France (Petronilla) in the Basilica of St. Peter's. The contract was signed August 27, 1498, the payment agreed upon 450 papal gold ducats, the work completed the following year. The Pietà stood always in St. Peter's but in different places: In 1537, the statue was moved to the Capella di Santa Maria della Febbre (Chapel of the Fever), sometime between 1572 and 1585 to the Choir of Sixtus IV, and finally, in 1749, to the Capella del Crocifisso, its present location.

In 1962, Pope John XXIII consented to the request of Francis Cardinal Spellman, Archbishop of New York, to have the Pietà brought to the New York World's Fair 1964-65, where it was seen by more than twenty-seven million visitors. It was enshrined in the Vatican Pavilion in a unique dark blue setting designed by Jo Mielziner, fully protected by bullet-proof glass—56 feet long and 27 feet high, in seven panels suspended from the ceiling—that sealed up the entire area of its exposition. Recordings of the beautiful Gregorian Chant by the Benedictine Monks of the Abbey of Saint-Pierre de Solesmes, France, (reflected from the huge surface of glass and giving the impression of coming from beyond the statue itself) animated this view with an unforgettable aura of contemplation. Its mission accomplished, the Pietà returned to St. Peter's, intact as it had left.

It should be noted that the poorly repaired fractures of Christ's little right finger and Mary's left fingers date back to 1736. Visible in my photographs are also black and white marks. The black ones are partly impurities (iron spots) in the marble, partly dirt as it accumulated through the centuries. (The statue was cleaned with pure, distilled water in 1973). The white marks are light reflections from the highly polished surface. The hole in the back of Christ's head and the metal fixtures on Mary's (removed in 1973) were inflicted during the last century to support metal halos. At probably the same time the statue was also placed on a wedge-like plaster base, tilting it so as to give it a more upright position. This base was removed in October 1965, on which occasion I photographed the view from the underside. The line across Mary's forehead is the edge of a coif.

On Pentecost Sunday, May 21, 1972, some twenty-five minutes before the Papal Benediction at noon, a madman diabolically attacked the statue with a hammer and, before he could be apprehended, inflicted upon it fifteen blows. Some of these mutilated the face of the Blessed Virgin, extinguishing the matchless beauty created by Michelangelo. Thanks to modern technology and the dedicated labors of the Vatican Museums' experts, the statue was restored to the highest possible degree of perfection and unveiled anew in its radiant splendor on March 25, 1973.

THE STORY OF THE PHOTOGRAPHS

All photographs, except those in the Appendix, were taken at the World's Fair, some during the preparations for the statue's crating. Having been responsible for the recorded music heard in the Vatican Pavilion—this through my close association with the Pius X School of Liturgical Music of Manhattanville College, N.Y., and at the request of the Archdiocese of New York—I was in the fortunate position to photograph the statue from angles never before seen. The stunning view from above on p. 33, for instance, I photographed one night through the opening of a lighting fixture in the ceiling; the picture on p. 32 was taken from a platform during the crating. In my effort (April 1964) to obtain the most beautiful picture of the Pietà for the Pavilion's souvenir record, I began this work of love. But once I had started, I could not stop until the ship carrying the statue back to Italy (November 1965) vanished from my sight.

I took thousands of pictures—in color and black and white, with large and small cameras, with lenses from 35 to 400mm, using the Pavilion lighting and my own, photographing from every angle at any hour of the day and the night. It was an experience that cannot be put into words, the experience of being in the presence of the mystery of true greatness. It was not new to me, for I was reminded

of Arturo Toscanini, whose rehearsals and performances I had attended for twenty years, a man as great in his field as Michelangelo in his —the one carving in stone, the other in fleeting sound. And so, as I spent countless hours in these devoted labors of photography, the statue became to me an ever-deeper mystery of beauty and faith, and I was struck by the realization that Michelangelo's greatest masterpiece had really never been seen in its full magnitude, except by a very privileged few.

In January 1973, I conceived the idea of reproducing some of my photographs in the original size of the statue (as far as a three-dimensional view can be represented by a two-dimensional picture). I was enabled to do so through the kindness of Dr. Deoclecio Redig de Campos, Director General of the Vatican's Monuments, Museums and Pontifical Galleries, and Dr. Vittorio Federici, Director of the Department for Scientific Research, in charge of the Pietà's restoration, who graciously provided me with many detailed measurements (e.g. Christ's left foot is 9.7 inches) and to whom I express here heartfelt gratitude. It is my intention to include a number of these "life-size" photographs in an appropriately large volume, of which this book is a *miniature version*.

On the last page, next to the restored arm, is a picture of one of these "life-size" photographs (p.60), compared with the statue's plaster cast in the Vatican made in 1933-34 and used for the restoration. Noteworthy in this picture is Dr. Federici's discovery of a very clear "M" following the natural lines in Mary's palm—possibly a secret earlier signature of Michelangelo.

A CONTEMPLATION

During all those years there stood by me a friend, Charles Rich, a man of deep interior prayer and learning, whose profound insights opened my eyes to far beyond what they had seen and of which I had not read anywhere. I recorded as he spoke to me, and this is part of what he said:

There is so much in the Pietà that if you lived a thousand years and wrote a thousand books you can never express it. In other words, there is a divine quality in it. It must have been inspired, because how could a boy, twenty-four years old, create a work like that? You can't imagine how. It was a special grace from God. It is true, he had to be an artist, but art alone could not have made the Pietà. —The Pietà transforms you inwardly. A prayerful spirit comes over you. . . . Prayerfulness . . . it changes people.

The spiritual and the artistic have never been so perfectly blended. One is inseparable from the other; and the fact that both reached the same degree of depth and intensity and mastery in one person, that is the essence which makes Michelangelo unique. What makes the Blessed Virgin remarkable is that it is his whole love of her that is in that face. You get an idea of what Michelangelo was by looking at that face—not what the Blessed Virgin was, but the faith that was in him to have ever done that. You couldn't describe her in words better than that face does. In fact you can't describe her in words, that is, that ineffable expression. It tells you more about Michelangelo than anything else. This is his tremendousness, excelling even the Sistine Chapel. The Sistine Chapel reveals artistic grandeur. The Pietà portrays simple faith. There is sanctity in that statue.

Every time we look at the Pietà the startling quality of the figure of Christ becomes more startling. As we look at it with devotion and love, the soul is made to feel that this is the Christ, the God Who became Man out of love for the human race. All the sorrows we can experience in this life are assuaged by looking at the Pietà. How we should love the Florentine sculptor for having given to the world so glorious a work! Michelangelo's statue is a ray from heaven, giving us a glimpse of the beauty awaiting us when we get there.

Robert Hupka

New York, March 6, 1975

LA PIETÀ

La parola *Pietà* deriva dal latino *pietas*, e significa "fedeltà al più alto grado . . . un amore profondo che nè vita nè morte posson distruggere." Il significato classico della parola *pietà* è sottomissione di tutta l'anima alla volontà di Dio, ma è anche il nome tradizionalmente dato alle opere d'arte che rappresentano Gesù morto nelle braccia di Sua Madre.

DATI STORICI

Michelangelo Buonarroti, che nacque a Caprese, vicino a Firenze il 6 marzo 1475 e che morì a Roma il 18 febbraio 1564, scolpì quattro Pietà. Questo volume è dedicato alla sua prima Pietà, la più famosa. La statua, alta cm.174, scolpita in un unico blocco di marmo bianco di Carrara fu ordinata dal Cardinale Jean de Bilhères de Lagraulas di St. Denis, Ambasciatore francese presso la Santa Sede, per la Cappella (Petronilla) dei Re Francesi nella Basilica di San Pietro. Il contratto fu firmato il 27 agosto 1498, il pagamento fu fissato a 450 ducati papali d'oro, e il lavoro fu completato l'anno seguente. La Pietà rimase sempre in San Pietro, ma in varie cappelle. Nel 1537 la statua fu spostata nella Cappella di Santa Maria della Febbre, tra il 1572 e il 1585 nel Coro di Sisto IV, e finalmente nel 1749 nella Cappella del Crocifisso, dove si trova attualmente.

Nel 1962 il Papa Giovanni XXIII accolse la richiesta del Cardinale Spellman, Arcivescovo di New York, di far trasportare la Pietà alla Fiera Mondiale di New York 1964-65, dove fu ammirata da oltre ventisette milioni di persone.

Era esposta nel Padiglione del Vaticano in un incomparabile ambiente blu scuro disegnato da Jo Mielziner, completamente protetta da vetrate blindate -lunghe m.17 e alte m.8, in sette pannelli sospesi dal soffitto- che coprivano l'intera superficie della mostra. Bellissimi canti gregoriani, incisi dai Monaci Benedettini dell'Abbazia di Saint-Pierre de Solesmes, Francia (la musica veniva riflessa dall'enorme superficie di vetro e sembrava provenisse dal retro della statua) riempivano la scena di un indimenticabile aura di contemplazione. Finita la sua missione, la Pietà fu riportata a San Pietro, intatta come ne era partita.

Bisogna notare che le riparazioni mal fatte nel mignolo del Cristo e nelle dita della mano sinistra della Madonna risalgono al 1736. Nelle mie fotografie sono anche visibili delle macchie nere e bianche. Quelle nere sono o impurità (macchie di ferro) nel marmo o sporcizia accumulatasi durante i secoli. (La statua fu ripulita con acqua distillata nel 1973.) Le macchie bianche sono riflessi di luce provenienti dalla superficie altamente levigata. Il buco nel retro della testa del Cristo e i supporti di metallo sulla testa della Madonna (tolti nel 1973) nel secolo scorso servirono per sostenere delle aureole di metallo. Probabilmente allo stesso tempo la statua fu anche posta su una base di gesso per inclinarla leggermente, dandole così una posizione più eretta. Questa base venne tolta nell'ottobre 1965 e fu allora che potei fotografare la parte inferiore della statua. La linea che attraversa la fronte di Maria è il lembo di una cuffia.

Il 21 maggio 1972, domenica di Pentecoste, più o meno venticinque minuti prima della benedizione papale, a mezzogiorno, un pazzo attaccò diabolicamente la statua con un martello e, prima di esser arrestato, inflisse alla statua ben quindici colpi. Alcuni di essi mutilarono il viso della Madonna, distruggendone l'incomparabile bellezza creata da Michelangelo. Grazie alla tecnologia moderna e al dedicato lavoro degli esperti dei Musei Vaticani, la statua fu restaurata al più alto grado di perfezione possibile e fu nuovamente svelata in tutto il suo splendore il 25 marzo 1973.

STORIA DELLE FOTOGRAFIE

Tutte le fotografie, eccetto quelle dell'appendice, furono fatte all'Esposizione Mondiale, alcune durante la preparazione dell'imballaggio della statua. Siccome mi sono personalmente occupato della registrazione della musica suonata nel Padiglione Vaticano, dati i miei stretti rapporti con la Scuola di Musica Liturgica Pio X del Manhattanville College, N.Y., e dietro richiesta dell'Arcivescovo di New York, mi trovai nella fortunata posizione di poter fotografare la statua da angoli mai veduti prima. Per esempio, la magnifica veduta presa dall'alto a pag.33 fu fotografata una notte dal soffitto attraverso un'apertura ricavatavi per una lampada. La fotografia a pag. 32 fu presa da una piattaforma durante l'imballaggio. Nel mio sforzo di ottenere la più bella fotografia della Pietà per il disco-ricordo del Padiglione (aprile 1964) iniziai con amore questo lavoro. Ma, una volta cominciato non potevo più smettere sino a quando il bastimento che riportava la statua in Italia (novembre 1965) sparì dalla mia vista.

Ho preso migliaia di fotografie, in colore e in bianco e nero, con macchine grandi e piccole, con lenti da mm. 35 a 400, usando le luci del Padiglione e le mie, fotografando da ogni angolo, a tutte le ore del giorno e della notte. E stata un'esperienza che non può esprimersi a parole, l'esperienza di essere davanti al mistero della vera grandezza. Non era del tutto nuova perchè mi ricollegava ad Arturo Toscanini che avevo seguito di presenza per venti anni assistendo alle sue prove e presentazioni: un gigante nel suo campo come Michelangelo nel suo—questi scolpendo nella pietra,

quello nel suono fuggevole. Così, mentre passavo innumerevoli ore in questo devoto lavoro, la statua si trasformò per me in un mistero anche più profondo di bellezza e di fede; e mi resi conto che il grande capolavoro di Michelangelo non era mai stato veramente capito nella sua vera grandezza, tranne che da pochissimi privilegiati.

Nel gennaio 1973 decisi di riprodurre alcune fotografie nella misura originale della statua (per quanto sia possibile riprodurre una veduta a tre dimensioni in una fotografia a due dimensioni). Mi fu possibile grazie alla gentilezza del Dott. Deoclecio Redig de Campos, Direttore Generale dei Monumenti, Musei e Gallerie del Vaticano, e del Dott. Vittorio Federici, Direttore del Gabinetto di Ricerche Scientifiche, incaricato del restauro della statua. Essi mi fornirono molte misure dettagliate ed a loro devo la mia eterna riconoscenza. (p.e. la misura del piede di Cristo è di cm.24,7). È mia intenzione includere alcune di queste fotografie a "grandezza naturale" in un appropriato grande volume, di cui questo libro è una *versione in miniatura*.

Nell'ultima pagina, accanto alla fotografia del braccio restaurato, c'è la riproduzione di una delle mie fotografie nella misura originale (pag. 60), vicino alla statua, che è una copia in gesso in possesso del Vaticano fatta nel 1933-34 ed usata per il restauro. Degna di nota in questa fotografia è la scoperta del Dott. Federici di un chiarissimo "M" che segue le linee naturali della palma della Madonna, forse un' anteriore firma segreta di Michelangelo.

UNA CONTEMPLAZIONE

Durante tutti questi anni ho avuto accanto un amico, Charles Rich, uomo di profonda vita interiore e saggezza, la cui acuta introspezione mi ha aperto maggiormente gli occhi e che mi ha detto delle cose che non ho mai letto altrove. Ho registrato quello che mi ha detto e riporto qui alcune delle sue osservazioni:

C'è tanta ricchezza nella Pietà che se uno vivesse mille anni e scrivesse mille libri mai la potrebbe esprimere. In altre parole, in questa statua c'è una certa qualità divina. Deve essere stata ispirata; altrimenti, come avrebbe potuto un giovane di ventiquattro anni creare un'opera simile? È impensabile. È stata una grazia speciale di Dio. È vero che ci voleva un artista, ma l'arte sola non avrebbe potuto produrre la Pietà.—La Pietà ci trasforma internamente. Lo spirito di preghiera ci invade. . . . spirito di preghiera. . . . questo trasforma gli uomini.

Mai la spiritualità e l'arte sono state così perfettamente in armonia, l'una inseparabile dall'altra e ambedue allo stesso grado di profondità, di intensità e di maestria in una persona—questa è l'essenza della grandezza unica di Michelangelo. Quello che rende straordinaria la Santa Vergine è il fatto che il suo viso rivela tutto l'amore di Michelangelo per Lei. Il viso della Vergine non ci rivela tanto quello che fu la Vergine quanto quello che fu Michelangelo —e cioè la fede che lo ispirava. Nessuna parola potrebbe descrivere la Vergine meglio che questo viso. Infatti non si può descrivere a parole quell'ineffabile espressione. Essa ci rivela di Michelangelo più che qualsiasi altra cosa. Questo è la sua terribilità, anche maggiore che nella Cappella Sistina. La Cappella Sistina rivela grandezza artistica. La Pietà riproduce semplice fede. C'è santità in questa statua.

Ogni volta che guardiamo la Pietà l'aspetto impressionante della figura del Cristo diventa più impressionante. Quando lo guardiamo con devozione e amore, la nostra anima sente che questo è il Cristo, il Dio che si fece uomo per amore degli uomini. Tutti i dolori che potremo soffrire in questa vita sono mitigati contemplando la Pietà. Come dovremmo amare lo scultore fiorentino per aver dato al

mondo un'opera così stupenda! La statua di Michelangelo è un vero raggio proveniente dal cielo che ci lascia intravedere le bellezze che ci attendono quando arriveremo lassù.

Robert Hupka
Tradotto da Anne M. Funaro
e Joseph H. Finlay

New York, 6 marzo, 1975

LA PIETÀ

Pietà, en italien, signifie "pitié, compassion, douleur." Le mot vient du latin *pietas,* et voulait dire "loyauté absolue . . . un amour profond que ni la vie ni la mort ne pouvait détruire." Le sens classique du mot *pietà* implique une soumission totale de l'âme à la Volonté divine, mais il désigne également les oeuvres d'art qui représentent le Christ après sa mort dans les bras de sa mère.

HISTORIQUE

Michel-Ange (Michelangelo Buonarroti) naquit à Caprese, près de Florence, le 6 mars 1475 et mourut à Rome le 18 février 1564. Il sculpta quatre Pietà. Ce volume est consacré à la première et à la plus célèbre d'entre elles. Cette sculpture, haute de 1,74m, faite d'un seul bloc de marbre blanc de Carrare, fut commandée à Michel-Ange par le cardinal Jean de Bilhères de Lagraulas de St. Denis, ambassadeur de France auprès du Saint-Siège, pour la chapelle des rois de France (Petronilla) à la basilique de Saint-Pierre. Le contrat fut signé le 27 août 1498 : Michel-Ange recevait 450 ducats pontificaux en or et s'engageait à exécuter le travail en un an. En 1537, la Pietà fut transférée d'abord à la Capella della Febbre (chapelle de la Fièvre) puis, entre 1572 et 1585, au choeur de Sixte IV et enfin, en 1749, à la Capella del Crocifisso (chapelle de la Crucifixion) où elle se trouve actuellement, toutes ces chapelles se trouvant dans la basilique de Saint-Pierre.

En 1962, à la demande du cardinal Spellman, arche-vêque de New York, le pape Jean XXIII acceptait d'envoyer la Pietà à la foire de New York 1964-65, où plus de vingt-sept millions de visiteurs purent la voir. Elle fut exposée au pavillon du Vatican dans un cadre unique, bleu foncé, conçu par Jo Mielziner, et protégée par une vitre à l'épreuve des balles—de 17 mètres de long et 8 mètres de large, divisée en sept panneaux suspendus au plafond—qui fermait complètement l'aire entière où elle était exposée. De magnifiques chants grégoriens, enregistrés par les bénédictins de Saint-Pierre de Solesmes en France, et réfléchis par l'immense surface de la vitre, ce qui donnait l'impression que le son venait de derrière la statue, ajoutaient à la scène une atmosphère de contemplation inoubliable. Sa mission accomplie, la Pietà retrouva sa place à Saint-Pierre, intacte comme avant son départ.

Il convient de noter que les cassures mal réparées du petit doigt de la main droite du Christ et des doigts de la main gauche de la Vierge remontent à 1736. On peut aussi voir sur mes photos des marques noires et des marques blanches. Les marques noires proviennent soit d'impuretés dans le marbe (taches ferrugineuses), soit de l'accumulation de poussière au cours des siècles. (La statue a été nettoyée en 1973 à l'eau distillée). Les marques blanches sont des réflections de lumière venant du fait que la surface du marbre est remarquablement polie. Le trou à l'arrière de la tête du Christ et les supports métalliques sur celle de Marie (retirés en 1973) servirent au siècle dernier à installer des auréoles métalliques au-dessus de la tête des personnages. Probablement à ce moment-là, la statue fut placée sur un socle de plâtre en forme de coin, l'inclinant de façon à lui donner une position plus droite. Ce socle fut retiré en octobre 1965, et je profitai de cette occasion pour prendre une photo de la sculpture par en-dessous. La ligne apparente sur le front de Marie est le bord d'une coiffe.

Le jour de la Pentecôte, le 21 mai 1972, environ vingt-cinq minutes avant la bénédiction papale de midi, un fou frappa diaboliquement la statue avec un marteau, et avant qu'on ait pu l'arrêter, il lui avait infligé quinze coups. Quelques-uns atteignirent le visage de la Vierge Marie, détruisant l'incomparable beauté créée par Michel-Ange. Néanmoins les ressources de la technologie moderne et le dévouement des experts des musées du Vatican permirent de restaurer la statue à un point étonnant de perfection et de la montrer à nouveau au public le 25 mars 1973.

COMMENTAIRES SUR LES PHOTOGRAPHIES

Toutes les photographies, sauf celles de l'appendice, furent prises à la foire de New-York, certaines pendant qu'on préparait l'emballage de la statue. Etant responsable des enregistrements musicaux au pavillon du Vatican—cela grâce à mes étroites relations avec l'école Pie X de musique sacrée au collège de Manhattanville, N.Y., et à la demande de l'archidiocèse de New York—j'eus ainsi la chance de pouvoir photographier la statue sous des angles absolument nouveaux. Par exemple, l'étonnante vue de dessus, p.33, fut prise une nuit par l'ouverture d'une lampe dans le plafond; la photo de la p.32 fut prise d'une plateforme quand on emballait la statue. C'est ainsi que je me mis ardemment au travail (avril 1964) dans l'intention d'obtenir la plus belle photo de la Pietà pour le disque souvenir du pavillon du Vatican. Mais une fois lancé dans cette tâche, je ne pus plus m'interrompre jusqu'au moment où le navire qui ramenait la statue en Italie (novembre 1965) eût disparu de ma vue.

J'ai pris des milliers de photos—en couleur et en noir et blanc, avec de grands et de petits appareils, avec des objectifs de 35 à 400 mm, en utilisant les lumières du pavillon ou mes propres projecteurs, la photographiant sous tous les angles à toutes les heures du jour et de la nuit. Cette expérience ne saurait être décrite par des mots, je me trouvais en présence du mystère de la vraie grandeur. Cela n'était pas nouveau pour moi, cela me rappelait les répétitions et les concerts d'Arturo Toscanini auxquels j'avais assisté pendant vingt ans, et dans son domaine Toscanini est un géant de l'envergure d'un Michel-Ange—l'un sculptant la pierre, l'autre sculptant les sons fugitifs. Et ainsi, tandis que je consacrais d'innombrables heures à ce travail de photographie, la statue devint pour moi un mystère toujours plus grand de beauté et de foi et je fus frappé par l'idée que le chef-d'oeuvre de Michel-Ange n'avait jamais été vraiment vu dans toute sa grandeur, si ce n'est par un petit nombre de privilégiés.

En janvier 1973, j'ai eu l'idée de tirer quelques-unes de mes photos aux dimensions mêmes de la statue (dans la mesure où une reproduction à deux dimensions peut représenter une statue à trois dimensions). J'ai pu mener à bien ce projet grâce à l'amabilité du Dr. Deoclecio Redig de Campos, Directeur général des monuments, musées et galeries du Vatican, et du Dr. Vittorio Federici, Directeur du Cabinet pour la recherche scientifique, chargé de la restauration de la Pietà, qui m'ont généreusement fourni de nombreuses mensurations (par exemple, le pied gauche du Christ mesure 24,7cm) et auxquels je tiens à exprimer ici tous mes sentiments de gratitude. J'ai l'intention de publier un certain nombre de ces photographies "grandeur nature" dans un volume de grandes dimensions dont ce livre est une *version en miniature.*

A la dernière page, près du bras restauré, figure une reproduction d'une des photographies grandeur nature (p.60), afin de permettre la comparaison avec le moulage en plâtre de la statue fait en 1933-34, qui se trouve au Vatican et qui fut utilisé pour la restauration. On remarquera sur cette photographie la découverte faite par le docteur Federici d'un "M" très visible suivant les lignes naturelles de la paume de la main de Marie—peut-être une ancienne signature secrète de Michel-Ange.

CONTEMPLATION

Durant toutes ces années, quelqu'un s'est tenu à mes côtés, Charles Rich, un homme animé d'une vie intérieure intense et possédant une grande culture. Ses idées profondes m'ont ouvert les yeux bien au delà de ce qu'ils avaient pu voir. Il m'a dit, et voici une partie de ses propos, que j'ai enregistrés directement et que je n'ai jamais vus imprimés nulle part:

Il y a tant de choses dans cette Pietà que même si vous viviez mille ans et écriviez mille livres, vous ne pourriez jamais tout exprimer. En d'autres termes, il y a là une qualité divine. Comment un jeune homme de vingt-quatre ans aurait-il pu créer une oeuvre pareille sans l'inspiration du ciel ? Cela ne se concevrait pas. C'est là une grâce spéciale de Dieu. Certes, il fallait que Michel-Ange fût un artiste, mais l'art seul n'aurait pas suffi à faire la Pietà—La contemplation de l'oeuvre vous transforme interieurement. Un esprit de prière s'empare de vous. . . . Le recueillement . . . l'homme en est transformé.

Le spirituel et l'artistique n'ont jamais été si parfaitement mêlés. Ils sont inséparables et le fait que l'un et l'autre ont atteint le même degré de profondeur et d'intensité, que cette maîtrise se trouve réunie en un seul homme, est essentiellement ce qui rend Michel-Ange unique. La Sainte Vierge est remarquable en ce que tout l'amour qu'il éprouvait pour elle est apparent dans son visage. En regardant ce visage, on peut se faire une idée de ce qu'était Michel-Ange—non de ce qu'était la Sainte Vierge—car on y voit la foi qu'il avait pour avoir accompli un tel ouvrage. Aucun

mot ne pourrait mieux la décrire que ce visage. En fait, cette ineffable expression ne saurait être rendue par des mots. Rien ne pourrait mieux vous faire comprendre Michel-Ange. Sa grandeur ici surpasse même celle de la Chapelle Sixtine. La Chapelle Sixtine montre la grandeur de l'artiste. La Pietà révèle sa foi dans sa simplicité. Il y a de la sainteté dans cette statue.

Chaque fois que nous regardons la Pietà, l'étonnante qualité de la figure du Christ devient plus remarquable. Nous le contemplons avec amour et dévotion, et l'âme sent alors que c'est bien là le Christ, le Dieu qui s'est fait homme pour l'amour de l'humanité. Tous les chagrins de la vie s'apaisent quand on regarde la Pietà. Que d'amour nous devons au sculpteur florentin pour avoir donné au monde un pareil chef d'oeuvre ! La statue de Michel-Ange est un rayon tombé du ciel, nous donnant l'idée de la beauté qui nous attend quand nous serons là-haut.

Robert Hupka
Traduit par Jacqueline Sareil

New York, le 6 mars 1975.

DIE PIETÀ

Pietà, ein italienisches Wort, "Mitleid," "Erbarmung," "Leid" bedeutend, stammt vom lateinischen *pietas*, "Treue in endlosem Masse, . . . eine tiefe Liebe, die weder Leben noch Tod zerstören kann." Die klassische Bedeutung des Wortes *pietà* ist die Ergebenheit in Gottes Willen mit ganzer Seele. Es ist auch die traditionelle Bezeichnung von Kunstwerken, die den Leichnam Christi in den Armen seiner Mutter darstellen.

HISTORISCHE DATEN

Michelangelo Buonarroti wurde in Caprese bei Florenz am 6.März 1475 geboren und starb in Rom am 18.Februar 1564. Er schuf vier Pietàs. Dieses Buch ist der ersten und berühmtesten gewidmet. Die 174 cm hohe Statue, gemeisselt aus einem Block weissen Carrara-Marmors, wurde von Kardinal Jean de Bilhères de Lagraulas von St. Denis, dem französischen Botschafter beim päpstlichen Stuhl, für die Kapelle der Könige von Frankreich (Petronilla) in der St.Peter-Basilika in Auftrag gegeben. Der Vertrag wurde am 27.August 1498 unterzeichnet; als Preis einigte man sich auf 450 päpstliche Golddukaten; im nächsten Jahr war das Werk vollendet. In 1537 wurde die Pietà in die Capella di Santa Maria della Febbre (Fieber-Kapelle), zwischen 1572 und 1585 in den Chor Sixtus' IV und schliesslich 1749 in die Capella del Crocifisso übertragen, wo sie seither steht.

In 1962 entsprach Papst Johann XXIII der Bitte des Kardinals Francis Spellman, Erzbischof von New York, die Pietà zu der New Yorker Weltausstellung 1964-65 bringen zu lassen, wo sie von mehr als siebenundzwanzig Millionen Besuchern gesehen wurde. Sie war im vatikanischen Pavillon in einer einzigartigen dunkelblauen Umfassung aufgestellt, entworfen von dem Bühnenarchitekten Jo Mielziner, völlig geschützt durch ein siebenteiliges, vom Plafond hängendes, kugelsicheres Glas -17 Meter lang und 8 Meter hoch- das den ganzen Raum ihrer Ausstellung abschloss. Tonaufnahmen des herrlichen Gregorianischen Gesanges der Benediktinermönche der Abtei Saint-Pierre de Solesmes, Frankreich, (rücktönend von der riesigen Glasfläche, als käme die Musik vom Hintergrund der Statue) beseelten dieses Bild mit einer unvergesslichen Stimmung der Andacht. Nach der Beendigung ihrer Mission kehrte die Pietà im selben Zustand, in dem sie Rom verlassen hatte, nach St. Peter zurück.

Es ist bemerkenswert, dass die schlecht reparierten Brüche des kleinen rechten Fingers Christi und die der linken Finger Marias auf 1736 zurückgehen. In meinen Photographien sind auch schwarze und weisse Flecke sichtbar. Die schwarzen sind teilweise Unreinheiten (Eisenflecke) im Marmor, teilweise durch Jahrhunderte angesammelter Schmutz. (Die Statue wurde 1973 mit destilliertem Wasser gereinigt.) Die weissen Flecke sind Spiegelungen der hochpolierten Oberfläche. Das Loch im Haupte Christi und die Metallträger auf dem Haupte Marias (beseitigt 1973) wurden der Statue während des letzten Jahrhunderts für Stützen von Heiligenscheinen hinzugefügt. Wahrscheinlich wurde die Statue zur selben Zeit auch auf einen keilartigen Gips-Sockel gesetzt, um ihr eine aufrechtere Stellung zu geben. Dieser Sockel wurde im Oktober 1965 beseitigt, wobei ich die Gelegenheit hatte, die Unterseite der Statue zu photographieren. Die Linie durch Marias Stirne ist der Rand einer Haube.

Am Pfingstsonntag, 21.Mai 1972, ungefähr fünfundzwanzig Minuten vor dem päpstlichen Mittags-Segen, stürzte sich ein Wahnsinniger geradezu teuflisch auf die Statue und fügte ihr, bevor er festgenommen werden konnte fünfzehn Hammerschläge zu. Einige dieser Schläge verstümmelten das Antlitz Marias und zerstörten die beispiellose Schönheit, die Michelangelo geschaffen hatte. Dank moderner Technologie und der hingebenden Arbeit der Fachleute der vatikanischen Museen gelang es, die Statue im höchstmöglichen Masse der Vollendung wiederherzustellen. Am 25.März 1973 wurde sie in ihrer strahlenden Pracht wieder enthüllt.

DIE GESCHICHTE DER PHOTOGRAPHIEN

Ich machte alle Aufnahmen, mit Ausnahme jener im Anhang, während der Weltausstellung und einige, als die Verpackung der Statue vorbereitet wurde. Dank meiner nahen Verbindung mit der Pius X.-Schule für Liturgische Musik des Manhattanville College, N.Y., und auf Ansuchen der Erzdiözese von New York, wurde ich mit den Tonaufnahmen der im vatikanischen Pavillon wiedergegebenen Musik betraut. In dieser bevorzugten Stellung war es mir möglich, die Statue von noch nie gesehenen Gesichtspunkten aus aufzunehmen. Die überwältigende Ansicht von oben (S.33), zum Beispiel, photographierte ich eines nachts durch einen Lampenausschnitt im Plafond; das Bild auf Seite 32 machte ich von einer Plattform während des Verpackens. In meinem Bemühen, das schönste Bild der Pietà für die Erinnerungs-Schallplatte des Pavillons (April 1964) aufzunehmen, fing ich dieses Liebeswerk an. Aber, einmal begonnen, konnte ich nicht mehr aufhören, bis das Schiff, das die Statue nach Italien zurücktrug (November 1965), meinem Blick entschwand.

Ich machte tausende von Aufnahmen—farbig, schwarz/weiss, mit grossen und kleinen Apparaten, mit 35-400mm Objektiven, die Lichtanlagen des Pavillons und meine eigenen benützend, von jedem möglichen Winkel und während jeder Tages- und Nachtstunde arbeitend. Es war ein Erlebnis, das nicht in Worten ausgedrückt werden kann, das Erlebnis, in der Gegenwart des Mysteriums wahrer Grösse zu sein. Dies war für mich nicht neu, da es mich an Arturo Toscanini erinnerte, dessen Proben und Aufführungen ich durch zwanzig Jahre beiwohnte, einen Mann, so gross auf seinem Gebiet wie Michelangelo auf seinem—der eine meisselte in Stein, der andere in verhallenden Tönen. Und so wurde die Statue, als ich zahllose Stunden in dieser aufopfernden photographischen Arbeit verbrachte, für mich ein immer tieferes Geheimnis von Schönheit und Glauben, und mich überwältigte die Erkenntnis, dass Michelangelos unvergleichliches Werk wirklich niemals in seiner vielfältigen Pracht gesehen worden war, mit Ausnahme von wenigen Bevorzugten.

Im Januar 1973 kam mir der Gedanke, einige meiner Photographien in der Originalgrösse der Statue wiederzugeben (soweit ein dreidimensionales Werk in einem zweidimensionalen Bild dargestellt werden kann). Dies wurde mir durch die Güte von Dr. Deoclecio Redig de Campos, Generaldirektor der vatikanischen Denkmäler, Museen und Galerien, und Dr. Vittorio Federici, dem Direktor der Abteilung für wissenschaftliche Forschungen und Leiter der Wiederherstellung der Pietà, ermöglicht, indem sie mir viele detaillierte Massangaben zukommen liessen (z.B. der linke Fuss Christi ist 24,7 cm lang), für die ich ihnen herzlich meine Dankbarkeit ausdrücke. Ich beabsichtige eine Anzahl solcher grossen Bilder in einem entsprechenden Prachtband zu veröffentlichen, von welchem das vorliegende Buch eine *Miniaturausgabe* ist.

Auf der letzten Seite, neben dem wiederhergestellten Arm, ist veranschaulicht, welchen Eindruck die Photographie auf S.60 in Originalgrösse macht, und zwar durch Vergleich mit dem Gipsabguss der Statue im Vatikan, der 1933-34 gegossen und bei der Wiederherstellung benützt wurde. Bemerkenswert in diesem Bilde ist Dr. Federicis Entdeckung eines sehr deutlichen "M", den natürlichen Linien in Marias Handfläche folgend—vielleicht eine geheime, frühere Signatur Michelangelos.

EINE BETRACHTUNG

In allen diesen Jahren stand mir ein Freund bei, Charles Rich, ein Mann tiefen innerlichen Gebetes, ein Weiser, dessen tiefe Erkenntnisse meine Augen weit über das, was sie sahen und wovon ich nirgends je gelesen hatte, aufschlossen. Ich machte Magnetofonaufnahmen, während er zu mir sprach, und hier ist ein Teil seiner Betrachtungen:

Es ist so viel in der Pietà, dass, wenn man auch tausend Jahre lebte und tausend Bücher schriebe, es nie erschöpfen kann. — Es ist, in anderen Worten, eine göttliche Eigenschaft in ihr. — Es muss Inspiration gewesen sein, wie hätte sonst ein junger, vierundzwanzigjähriger Mann ein solches Werk schaffen können? Man kann es sich nicht vorstellen. Es war eine besondere Gnade Gottes. Es ist wahr, er musste ein Künstler sein, aber Kunst allein konnte die Pietà nicht geschaffen haben. — Die Pietà verwandelt unser Inneres. Ein Gefühl der Andacht kommt über uns . . . . Andacht . . . sie verwandelt die Seele des Menschen.

Niemals wurden Geistiges und Künstlerisches so vollkommen und unzertrennlich vereint; und die Tatsache, dass beide denselben Grad von Tiefe, Intensität und Meisterschaft in einer Person erreichten, ist der Kern von Michelangelos Einzigartigkeit.

Was die Heilige Jungfrau so bemerkenswert macht,

ist, dass seine ganze Liebe zu ihr in diesem Gesicht ausgedrückt ist. Man bekommt einen Begriff, was Michelangelo war, wenn man dieses Gesicht betrachtet—nicht was die Heilige Jungfrau war, sondern der Glaube in ihm, der ihn dies schaffen liess. Worte können sie nicht besser schildern als dieses Gesicht. Wahrlich, man kann ihren unaussprechlichen Ausdruck nicht in Worte kleiden. Er sagt uns mehr über Michelangelo als irgend etwas anderes. Das ist seine ungeheure Erhabenheit, die sogar die Sixtinische Kapelle übertrifft. Die Sixtinische Kapelle offenbart künstlerische Grösse; die Pietà reinen Glauben. In dieser Statue ist Heiligkeit.

Jedesmal, wenn wir die Pietà betrachten, wird die erschütternde Figur Christi erschütternder. Wenn wir sie mit Inbrunst und Liebe ansehen, fühlt unsere Seele, dass dies Christus ist, der Gott, der aus Liebe zur Menschheit Mensch wurde. — Alle Schmerzen, die wir in diesem Leben ertragen können, werden gelindert, wenn wir die Pietà betrachten. — Wie sehr müssen wir den Florentiner Bildhauer lieben, dass er der Welt ein solch glorreiches Werk gegeben hat! Michelangelos Statue ist ein Strahl vom Himmel, der uns einen Schimmer der Schönheit gibt, die uns dort erwartet.

Robert Hupka

New York, 6. März 1975

LA PIETÁ

Pietá, es una palabra italiana que significa "piedad," "compasión," "dolor," deriva del latín *pietas*, significa una actitud de "lealtad en grado sumo. . . . . . profundo amor que ni la vida ni la muerte puede destruir." El clásico significado de la palabra *pietá* es todo lo animado sumido en la Voluntad Divina; y además se da tradicionalmente este nombre a las obras de arte que representan el cuerpo muerto de Cristo en los brazos de Su Madre.

DATOS HISTÓRICOS

Miguel Angel Buonarroti, nació en Capriese cerca de Florencia el 6 de marzo de 1475 y murió en Roma el 18 de febrero de 1564, esculpió cuatro Pietás. Este libro está dedicado a la primera y más famosa de ellas. De 174 cm. de altura está esculpida en un solo bloque de mármol blanco de Carrara, fue un encargo del Cardenal Jean Bilhères de Lagraulas de San Denis, Embajador francés ante la Santa Sede, para la Capilla de los Reyes de Francia (Petronilla) en la Basílica de San Pedro. Se firmó el contrato el 27 de agosto de 1498, el pago estipulado serían 450 ducados papales de oro, y el trabajo se terminó el siguiente año. La Pietá ha estado en diferentes lugares de San Pedro. En 1537 fué trasladada a la Capella de Santa Maria della Febbre (Capilla de la Fiebre), entre 1572 y 1585 al Coro de Sixto IV, y finalmente en 1749 a la Capella del Crocifisso, su actual ubicación.

En 1962, el Papa Juan XXIII accedió a la petición del Cardenal Francis Spellman, Arzobispo de Nueva York, de traer la Pietá a la Feria Mundial de Nueva York en los años de 1964-65, donde fué contemplada por más de veintisiete millones de visitantes. Se la colocó como una reliquia, en el Pabellón del Vaticano con un grandioso e inigualable fondo azul oscuro diseñado por Jo Mielziner. Esta área estaba completamente cerrada y protegida por siete paneles colgantes de cristal a prueba de balas, un total de 17 metros de largo y 8 metros de alto. Unas grabaciones del hermoso Canto Gregoriano de los Monjes Benedictinos de la Abadía de Saint-Pierre de Solesmes, en Francia, (el sonido se proyectaba contra la enorme superficie de cristal, dando la impresión de proceder de más allá de la misma estatua), daban vida a esta visión produciendo inolvidable aura de contemplación. Cumplida su misión, la Pietà regresó a San Pedro, intacta como había salido.

Debemos aclarar que las fracturas mal restauradas del dedo meñique de la mano derecha de Cristo y los dedos de la mano izquierda de la Virgen datan de 1736. En mis fotografías se observan unas manchas blancas y negras. Algunas de las negras son debidas a impurezas del mármol (manchas de hierro) y otras a suciedad acumulada por los siglos. (La estatua fue limpiada en 1973 con agua pura destilada.) Las manchas blancas son reflejos de la luz sobre la pulidísima superficie del mármol. El agujero en la parte posterior de la cabeza de Cristo y los soportes de metal en la de la Virgen (quitados en 1973) se hicieron en el siglo pasado para colocarles sendas diademas de metal. Probablemente por la misma época, la estatua quedó situada sobre una plataforma de yeso—en forma de cuña—para inclinarla un poco y darle una posición más esbelta. Esta base le fue retirada en octubre de 1965, y en esa ocasión yo tomé la foto desde abajo. La línea que cruza la frente de la Virgen es el borde de una cofia.

El domingo de Pentecostés, 21 de mayo de 1972, unos veinticinco minutos antes de la Bendición Papal del mediodía, un loco atacó diabolicamente a la estatua con un martillo, y antes que pudiera ser apresado, infligió sobre ella quince golpes. Algunos de ellos mutilaron el rostro de la Santísima Virgen, extinguiendo la inigualable belleza creada por Miguel Angel. Gracias a la tecnología moderna y al cuidadoso trabajo de los expertos de los Museos Vaticanos la estatua fue restaurada con el máximo grado de perfección posible y nuevamente expuesta en su radiante esplendor el 25 de marzo de 1973.

HISTORIA DE LAS FOTOGRAFÍAS

Todas las fotografías, excepto las del Apéndice, fueron tomadas en la Feria Mundial, algunas durante los preparativos para el embalaje de la estatua. Habiendo sido encargado de las grabaciones musicales que se escuchaban en el Pabellón del Vaticano—gracias a mi estrecho contacto con la Escuela Pío X de Música Litúrgica de Manhattanville College, N.Y., y a petición de la Archidiócesis de Nueva York—tuve una oportunidad privilegiada para fotografiar la escultura desde ángulos que nunca habían sido vistos antes. Por ejemplo, la sorprendente vista de alto de la p. 33, la tomé una noche desde el techo, a través de la abertura del foco de la luz; la fotografía de la p. 32 fue tomada desde una plataforma durante el embalaje. En mis esfuerzos por obtener la más hermosa fotografía de la Pietá para el disco-souvenir del Pabellón Vaticano (abril de 1964), empecé con amor este trabajo. Una vez que comencé no pude detenerme hasta que el barco que llevó la estatua de regreso a Italia (noviembre de 1965) se desvaneció ante mi vista.

Tomé literalmente, miles de fotografías, en color y en blanco y negro; con las cámaras más grandes y con las más pequeñas; con lentes desde 35 hasta 400 mm; usando la iluminación del Pabellón y la mía propia; fotografiando desde cada ángulo posible a cualquier hora del día y de la noche. . . . . . Fue una experiencia que no puede expresarse en palabras, la experiencia de estar en la presencia del misterio de una genuina grandiosidad. Esto no era nuevo para mí, pues me recordaba a Arturo Toscanini, a cuyos ensayos y actuaciones asistí durante 20 años, un hombre tan grande en su campo como Miguel Angel en el suyo: éste esculpía en piedra, aquél en el fugaz sonido. . . . . . Y a medida, que yo pasaba incontables horas en este fervoroso trabajo de las fotografías, la estatua se convertía para mí en un misterio aún más profundo de belleza y fe. Me emocionaba al comprender que la grandeza de esta obra maestra de Miguel Angel realmente nunca había sido vista en su total magnitud, excepto por unos pocos privilegiados.

En enero de 1973, concebí la idea de reproducir algunas de mis fotografías al tamaño natural de la escultura (hasta donde una imagen tridimensional pudiera ser representada por una fotografía bidimensional). Pude hacerlo gracias a la gentileza del Dr. Deoclecio Redig de Campos, Director General de los Monumentos, Museos y Galerías del Vaticano, y del Dr. Vittorio Federici, Director del Departamento de Investigaciones Científicas, a cuyo cargo estuvo la restauración de la Pietá, quienes amablemente me proporcionaron minuciosas medidas, (por ejemplo, el pie izquierdo de Cristo mide 24.7 cm.) por lo cual les estaré agradecido siempre de todo corazón. Es mi intención incluir un número de estas fotografías de "tamaño natural" en un gran libro apropiado para éso, del cual esta edición es una *versión miniatura*.

En la última página, junto al brazo restaurado, aparece una de las fotografías en su "tamaño original" (Pag. 60) puesta como comparación junto al vaciado en yeso existente en el Vaticano, hecho en 1933-34 y que fué usado para hacer la restauración. Es notable en esta fotografía el reciente descubrimiento que hizo el Dr. Federici de una clarísima "M" siguiendo las líneas naturales de la palma de la mano de la Virgen María—posiblemente una primera firma secreta de Miguel Angel.

UNA CONTEMPLACIÓN

Durante estos años ha estado muy cerca de mí un amigo, Charles Rich, hombre de profunda vida interior de oración y de cultura, cuya profunda percepción abrió mis ojos, más allá de lo que ellos habían visto y de lo que yo hubiera leído en ninguna parte. Mientras hablaba fui grabando sus palabras y esto es parte de lo que dijo:

Tiene tanto contenido la Pietá, que si uno viviera miles de años y escribiera miles de libros nunca podría expresarlo. . . . . Dicho de otro modo, hay algo casi divino en ella. . . . . Tiene que haber sido una obra inspirada; si no, ¿cómo es posible, que un joven de veinticuatro años, creara una obra como ésta?. No se puede comprender cómo. . . . . Fue una gracia especial de Dios. Es verdad, que el autor tenía que ser un artista, pero sólo el arte no pudo haber hecho la Pietá. . . . . La Pietá nos transforma interiormente. Un deseo de oración nos invade. Es el espíritu de oración . . . . . que transforma a las almas.

Lo espiritual y lo artístico nunca habían estado tan compenetrados. Lo uno es inseparable de lo otro; y el hecho que cada uno alcance igual grado de profundidad, intensidad y maestría en una sola persona, es en esencia lo que da a Miguel Angel su carácter excepcional. . . . . Lo que hace admirable a la Santísima Virgen es que está reflejado en ese rostro todo el amor que él sentía por Ella. Se capta la idea de lo qué fue Miguel Angel sólo contemplando esa cara. . . . . no tal como la Virgen fue, sino la fe que él tenía y que le hizo capaz de esta obra. No se podría describirla con palabras de un modo mejor a como lo hace ese rostro. . . . . De hecho no se puede describir en palabras esa inefable expresión. . . . . Nos dice más sobre Miguel Angel que ninguna otra obra. Esta es su mayor grandeza, que aún excede a la revelada en la Capilla Sixtina. En la Capilla Sixtina se despliega una innegable grandeza artística. La Pietá muestra una fe sencilla. Hay santidad en esa estatua.

Cada vez que miramos la Pietá, la figura de Cristo, en sí conmovedora se nos hace más estremecedora. Cuando la miramos con devoción y amor, el alma siente que Ese es el Cristo, el Dios hecho Hombre por amor a los hombres. . . . . Todos los sufrimientos que podamos sentir en esta vida se mitigan el contemplar la Pietá. . . . . ¡Cuánto debemos al escultor florentino por haberle dado al mundo tan gloriosa obra! La estatua de Miguel Angel es como un rayo de los cielos, que nos da sólo un destello de la belleza que allá nos espera.

Robert Hupka
Traducido por Marta de la Portilla

Nueva York, 6 de marzo de 1975

A PIETÀ

Pietà, palavra italiana que quer dizer "piedade", "compaixão", "pesar", vem do latim *pietas*, e significa "lealdade ao mais alto gráu . . . um amor profundo que nem a vida nem a morte podem destruir". O sentido clássico da palavra *pietà* é a conformidade total da alma com a vontade divina, mas é também o nome dado tradicionalmente às obras de arte que representam o corpo de Cristo morto nos braços de sua mãe.

DADOS HISTÓRICOS

Miguel Angelo Buonarroti nasceu em Caprese, perto de Florença, no dia 6 de março de 1475 e morreu em Roma no dia 18 de fevereiro de 1564. Ele esculpiu quatro Pietàs. Este livro é consagrado à primeira e mais famosa delas. A estátua, que mede 1,74m de altura, esculpida num só bloco de mármore branco de Carrara, foi encomendada pelo Cardeal Jean de Bilhères de Lagraulas de St. Denis, Embaixador da França junto à Santa Sé, para a Capela (Petronilla) dos reis de França na Basílica de São Pedro. O contrato foi assinado no dia 27 de agôsto de 1498, o pagamento ajustado em 450 ducados Papais de ouro, a obra terminada no ano seguinte. A Pietà permaneceu sempre na Basílica de São Pedro, mas em diferentes locais. Em 1537, a estátua foi removida para a Capela de Santa Maria della Febbre, entre 1572 e 1585 para o côro de Sixto IV e, finalmente, em 1749 para a Capela do Crucifixo, onde se encontra atualmente.

Em 1962, o Papa João XXIII aquiesceu ao pedido do Cardeal Francis Spellman, Arcebispo de Nova York, para trazer a Pietà para a Feira Mundial de Nova York em 1964-65, onde ela foi vista por mais de vinte e sete milhões de pessoas. Foi exposta no Pavilhão do Vaticano, num extraordinário cenário azul escuro desenhado por Jo Meilziner, protegida completamente por um vidro à prova de bala -17 metros de largura e 8 metros de altura, em sete painéis suspensos do teto- que fechava totalmente toda a área de sua exposição. A música gravada do belo Canto Gregoriano dos Monges Beneditinos da Abadia de Saint-Pierre de Solesmes, França (repercutida pelo enorme vidro e dando a impressão de vir de além da própria estátua), impregnava êste quadro de uma aura inesquecível de contemplação. Sua missão cumprida, a Pietà voltou para a Basílica de São Pedro tão intacta como quando partiu.

Deve-se mencionar que as fraturas mal restauradas do dedo mínimo esquerdo de Jesus e dos dedos esquerdos da Virgem datam de 1736. Marcas pretas e brancas são também visíveis nas minhas fotografias. As pretas são em parte impurezas (manchas de ferro) no mármore, em parte poeira acumulada através dos séculos. (A estátua foi limpa em 1973 com água pura destilada). As manchas brancas são leves reflexos do polimento intenso da superfície. O orifício na parte posterior da cabeça do Cristo e os dispositivos metálicos na da Virgem (removidos em 1973) foram feitos no século passado para sustentar auréolas metálicas. Provàvelmente na mesma época a estátua foi também colocada sôbre uma base de gesso em forma de cunha, que a inclinava para dar-lhe uma posição mais vertical. Esta base foi retirada em outubro de 1965, e nesta ocasião fiz a fotografia que mostra a estátua por baixo. A linha na testa da Virgem é a extremidade de uma touca.

No domingo de Pentecostes, no dia 21 de maio de

1972, uns vinte e cinco minutos antes da bênção papal do meio dia, um louco atacou diabòlicamente a estátua com um martelo e, antes que pudesse ser apreendido, deu umas quinze marteladas. Algumas delas mutilaram o rosto da Virgem, extinguindo a beleza sem par criada por Miguel Angelo. Graças à tecnologia moderna e ao trabalho dedicado dos especialista dos museus do Vaticano, foi restaurada ao mais alto gráu de perfeição possível e exposta de novo no seu radiante esplendor no dia 25 de março de 1973.

A HISTÓRIA DAS FOTOGRAFIAS

Tôdas as fotografias, com exceção das do Apêndice, foram feitas durante a Feira Mundial, algumas durante os preparativos para a embalagem da estátua. Tendo sido responsável pela música gravada ouvida no Pavilhão do Vaticano —através da minha estreita associação com a Escola de Música Litúrgica Piu X do Manhattanville College, N.Y., e a pedido da Arquidiocese de Nova York—eu me encontrei numa posição privilegiada que me permitiu fotografar a estátua de ângulos nunca vistos antes. A fotografia extraordinária tirada de cima, pp.33, por exemplo, fiz uma noite através da abertura de um aparelho para iluminação situado no teto; a fotografia na pág. 32 foi feita de uma plataforma durante a embalagem. No meu esfôrço (abril 1964) para obter a fotografia mais bonita da Pietà para o disco de lembrança do Pavilhão, comecei êste trabalho de amor. Mas, uma vez começado, não pude parar até que o navio levando a estátua de volta à Itália (novembro 1965) desaparecesse da minha vista.

Fiz milhares de fotografias -em cores e em branco e preto, com aparelhos grandes e pequenos, com lentes de 35 a 400 mm, usando a iluminação do Pavilhão e meus próprios projetores, fotografando de todo ângulo a tôda hora do dia e da noite. Foi uma experiência que não pode ser expressa com palavras, a experiência de estar na presença do mistério da verdadeira grandeza. Essa sensação não era nova para mim, pois me fazia lembrar Arturo Toscanini a cujos ensaios e apresentações assisti durante vinte anos, um homem tão grande em seu campo quanto Miguel Angelo no seu—um criando na pedra, outro com o som efêmero. E assim, tendo dedicado horas sem conta a êsse trabalho de fotografia, a estátua tornou-se para mim um mistério de beleza e fé cada vêz mais profundo e dei-me conta de que a maior obra-prima de Miguel Angelo só tinha sido vista em sua plena magnitude por uns poucos privilegiados.

Em janeiro de 1973 concebi a idéia de reproduzir algumas de minhas fotografias no tamanho natural da estátua (na medida em que um objeto em três dimensões possa ser representado por uma fotografia em duas dimensões). Isso me foi possível graças à bondade do Dr. Deoclécio Redig de Campos, Diretor Geral dos Monumentos, Museus e Galerias do Vaticano e do Dr. Vittorio Federici, Director do Gabinete de Pesquisa Científica, encarregado da restauração da Pietà, que gentilmente me forneceram muitas medidas detalhadas (o pé de Cristo, por exemplo, mede 24,7 cms.), e aos quais expresso perene gratidão. E minha intençao de incluir um número dessas fotografias em "tamanho natural" num grande volume apropriado para isto, do qual esta edição é uma versão miniatura. Na última página, ao lado do braço restaurado, está uma das minhas fotografias em "tamanho natural" (pág. 60) colocada para comparação junto ao modêlo da estátua em gesso que existe no Vaticano, feito em 1933-34 e usado para a restauração. Vale a pena notar nessa fotografia a descoberta do Dr. Federici de um perfeito "M" seguindo as linhas naturais da palma da mão da Virgem—talvez uma mais antiga assinatura secreta de Miguel Angelo.

CONTEMPLAÇÃO

Durante todos êsses anos tive o apoio de um amigo, Charles Rich, um homem erudito e de intensa vida interior cuja profunda penetração me fêz ver além do que os meus olhos tinham visto e me mostrou o que nunca tinha lido em parte alguma. O que segue é parte do que êle disse, gravado na medida em que me falava:

Há tanto na Pietà, que se se vivesse mil anos e se se escrevesse mil livros, não se poderia exprimi-lo. Em outras palavras, há uma qualidade divina nela. Deve ter sido inspirada porque, como poderia um jovem de vinte e quatro anos criar uma obra como esta? Não se pode imaginar como. Foi uma graça especial de Deus. É verdade, teria que ser um artista, mas a arte sòzinha não poderia ter feito a Pietà. A Pietà nos transforma interiormente. Um espírito de prece como que nos envolve . . . O recolhimento transforma a gente.

O espiritual e o artístico nunca estiveram tão perfeitamente unidos. Um é inseparável do outro; e o fato de que ambos atingiram o mesmo gráu de profundeza, intensidade e mestria numa só pessoa é a essência do caráter excepcional de Miguel Angelo. O que torna a Santa Virgem extraordinária é o fato de que o amor de Miguel Angelo por ela se encontra naquele rosto. Ao olhar-se aquele rosto tem-se uma idéia do que êle era, não o que a Virgem Maria era, mas a fé que levou o artista a fazê-lo assim. Não se pode descrever a Virgem melhor do que aquele rosto o faz. Na realidade, não se pode descrevê-lo com palavras, isto é, aquela expressão inefável. Ela revela mais sôbre Miguel Angelo do que qualquer outra coisa. Aqui o seu gênio supera até a Capela Sixtina. A Capela Sixtina revela grandeza artística. A Pietà retrata a fé simples. Há santidade nessa estátua.

Cada vêz que se olha a Pietà, a surpreendente qualidade da figura de Cristo se torna mais evidente. Olhando para ela com devoção e amor, a alma é levada a sentir que êste é o Cristo, o Deus que se tornou Homen por amor pela raça humana. Tôdas as dores que se sofre nesta vida são aliviadas pela contemplação da Pietà. Como deveríamos amar o escultor florentino por ter legado ao mundo obra tão gloriosa! A estátua de Miguel Angelo é um raio do céu que nos deixa vislumbrar a beleza que nos espera quando lá chegarmos.

Robert Hupka
Traduzido por Marcila Rainot

Nova York, 6 de março de 1975.